Review for *Through The Storm*

Through the storm is a very educative and enlightening book. It gave me a glimpse into the life of a woman, showing how it is daring for the gender to take a stand in the male-dominated industry. It also draws a line of similarity with most individual experiences of the 2020 pandemic. It is a good read with eye-opening, self-helping and self-developing ideas. It also exemplifies the use of faith in life.

—Katherine Peterson

THROUGH *The* STORM

Akaycia Marbury

info@akayciaskorner.com

ISBN:
Paperback: 979-8-98-73234-0-3
eBook: 979-8-9873234-1-0

Dedication:

I dedicate this book to all the black sheep of the family. To everyone who has been an outcast in their families for as long as they can remember. To the courageous individuals who dare to speak up when no one else will. To the strong-spirited individuals who know that they are meant to be a change agent, break generational curses, and stand strong against the norm. I want you to know that living in your purpose is always worth the sacrifice. We sacrifice being comfortable, being liked, and sometimes forfeit the love we desperately want because we have to. Many will not understand, learn to be ok with not being understood. You are worthy and you are exactly where you are supposed to be. I wrote this book for you. We can do this!!! We can build our weapons within to make it through the storm

Table of contents

Introduction

"You may not control all the events that happen to you,
but you can decide not to be reduced by them."

—Maya Angelou

A LETTER TO MY READERS:

First things first. If you are reading this book and you see some skeletons that are mentioned about you, please don't be upset. This book is not meant to shame or upset anyone. Please know it was not easy to be open. These feelings were like raw wounds. This writing was the medicine to make them less painful. It was not easy to share this story, my story. I almost didn't publish this book out of fear. God has led me to this point for a reason. With the great purpose that supersedes yours or my comfortability, I pray that you can see the purpose of me sharing so much of myself, so much of my pains. I needed to take this courageous step to not only begin to truly heal but hopefully to also encourage just one person to keep pushing through his/her storm. I see now that part of my purpose is to be for someone what I wish I had.

If you're reading this book, I want you to know you're not alone in the world. Many times, I've felt alone or lost and sometimes, inside a crowded room of people that look like me. I want you to know that I see you. You are the one always working overtime to pay your bills and survive each month. I see you. For the one who is working at a company that is short-staffed and underpaid, you can't afford to quit because your options are too few and far in between. I see you. This book is for the one who has been battling depression since the pandemic began or maybe even before the pandemic. You're too ashamed to admit out loud that you just don't quite feel like yourself anymore because people will or might judge. People will not believe your cries because you're the strong one. Although not visible, deep down, you are crying tears that have no end. I see you.

I see you because I have been and at times, still am you. I know what it's like to feel like you are carrying the burden of the world on your shoulders, to scream for help and everyone pretends that they don't hear you. I've been worn down and broken and tired working for a company that only knows me by a numerical number and expectation assigned to my name. I know what it's like to wear the mask of many because everyone expects something different from you to survive. I see you.

I decided to write about this phase of my life and journey for a few core reasons. First, I needed to begin to heal. Second, I wanted to take note of my learned lessons so that maybe someone would be encouraged, meaning this pain would not have been in vain. Third and maybe the most important, I know that there is someone on the edge, so close to giving up, and not a soul has any idea. Baby, this book is for you.

I've taken some incredible and courageous steps to become the woman of my dreams and the best possible version of myself. To be frank, it wasn't easy. It's still not easy. I am always at war with my old self. I had to bury my old habits and behaviors. I had to break up and detach myself from what I thought I wanted in my life. I began to dig deep within myself and do the work on the ugly parts of myself that scared me. The parts of myself that I never wanted anyone to see or know existed. I decided to take control of my life and turn things around for the better. I decided that I deserved to breathe.

Some of what I'm about to share with you in this book will probably stir up tears or make you feel angry, but hopefully, you will chuckle at my dry humor from time to time. My experiences are not monolithic to just me. I know other women who have worked through similar fires and got burned. Other women have chosen to suffocate themselves into tiny replicas of whom they used to be to survive. To those women, and many others, I hope my story inspires you to fight back. To change courses on the destination of your life. To lean into a greater understanding of whom God has called you to be in this journey. To love yourself through your hardships and sacrifices. To believe that love is possible for you again. To know that you are worthy of happiness while you are here on earth.

I have found peace in this journey, and now, I encourage you to do the same. Build your weapon within so you can make it through the storm.

Chapter One

The Pandemic

At the beginning of the pandemic, I had been in the Retail Industry for a few years. In 2020, I was a Retail 3 Operations Manager. My position required me to manage several day-to-day operations, not limited to our front-line staff, food safety, staff education, and development. Inclusive to this role was project management. At one point, my most involved project required me to be the culinary expert and develop lesson plans to teach first and second-year medical students and residents at the hospital I worked for. The objective was to teach them how to be more comfortable and confident in the kitchen so they would be more relatable in regard to helping their future patients stick to realistic nutrition goals.

I spent the majority of my time at work. My job consumed me. I dedicated my life to my career. I adjusted quickly to the long hours each day. In the process, I forfeited my social life and self-care.

My body began to ache from the long days and nights. I quickly began to grow exhausted mentally, physically, and spiritually. Just as the pandemic was beginning, my position was classified as an essential worker. It was a mental adjustment for me. I was constantly battling within myself with my contribution to the business. I soon realized that I would have to buckle up for the long ride ahead like many other people.

The pandemic impacted my industry immensely. Most of our daily sanitation practices needed to adapt to the new COVID-19 restrictions. In most cases, when an employee could not make it to work, we had to implement new protocols. The new protocols required immediate testing and quarantining of the workspace or department. This equated to fewer resources available on hand for day-to-day business. I was responsible for developing solutions and managing them.

I could feel the pressure to manage a crisis hanging on my shoulders. I began to experience an outer body awakening that caused me to mentally break down. I was no longer my former self. I began to suffocate under the immense pressure to rise above the obstacles and be everything to everyone else. I was drowning in my own blood, sweat, and tears. I had a meditation room that I would just breathe and cry in; I refused to let the rest of the world see my pain. I conditioned myself to suffer in silence. At the time, I thought I was keeping my weaknesses under control.

I wasn't myself, and I was quickly becoming someone I didn't recognize or like. Something within me began to cry out loud and ask God for help. I needed God, and I prayed for him to be my anchor and guide me back to His salvation. I was falling, and I was falling fast. I knew I could not make it on my own living inside my head. I was spiraling beyond my control.

God heard my cries and answered my prayers, but not in a pretty way. When you ask God for a specific prayer, be open to his answer! I had a panic attack at work and had to be rushed to the emergency room. Losing control over my body, I was terrified. It was in the hospital that I connected with a pastor. The pastor was very unassuming in his presence. He could have easily been dismissed as just another employee inside the hospital. With haze and confusion in my eyes, I was able to see past my own suffrage. I noticed him. I noticed a certain light in his eyes and his spirit. This pastor was meant to find himself in my hospital room. I always believed that God uses people to speak directly to us. I wasn't afraid to invite this angel in disguise inside my spirit or hospital room. I knew that our paths crossing was with reason. Through prayer, conversation, and the spirit of discernment, God revealed to me that my days of figuring things out on my own were behind me. No, my problems would not go away or get easier, but I was about to embark on a journey to become stronger. Take note that every encounter you have in this life is with purpose.

God sent the pastor into my life to pour words of encouragement into me. This pastor held my hand and embraced me with love and kindness. Genuine gestures that I have never been used to. He wouldn't let go of my hand. He spoke life into me as I lay inside the hospital bed. He knew exactly what to pray for, and each word hits its target. I began to fight back my tears. I didn't want the pastor to see that part of me. I didn't want to look weak. But the look in his eyes and the nod of his head permitted me to let go of all the pain and burden I'd been carrying on the inside. I didn't realize it then, but God had given me a spiritual rinse. The pain was weighing me down and destroying me. God needed unfiltered access to me, and I had been standing in my own way all this time. At that moment, I found hope on the other side of my pain.

I realized that I was holding on to a version of myself that God could no longer use. God wanted to upgrade me and guide me to the next level of my calling, my purpose. I had been too busy. I overextended myself and gave all my energy to the things that didn't serve my greater good. At that moment, I found the strength and courage to trust in God through every storm. I realized that what I was viewing as my weakness was really the power I was running from.

***

After the hospital, my life at work was no longer the same. The pandemic was in full swing. The world around me seemed abnormal. We were under strict restrictions in the workplace to help prevent the spread of the virus. Social distancing became the normative practice in every department. I began to adjust to life underneath a mask and washing my hands frequently throughout the day.

It was only a few months later when the inevitable happened. Layoffs and downsizing were beginning to happen across the country. The virus had led to many people losing their jobs, businesses shutting down, and children being designated to virtual school. Before I could fully wrap my mind around everything happening, suddenly, I found myself on the other side of the pandemic.

Our corporate offices decided it was best for the business to begin layoffs. I was notified in June that my position would be eliminated. My term as an employee would be effective up until July 17th, 2020.

The news of being laid off caused me to go numb. I couldn't believe I wouldn't have a secure job any longer. I felt lost and overwhelmed by the sudden news. That day, I pretended to be fine. I smiled and carried on. At the end of my shift, I gathered my belongings, sat inside my truck, took a deep breath, and began to cry.

I asked God, "What am I going to do now?"

I'd been employed with the company for almost five years. I'd become accustomed to working every day and getting a paycheck every two weeks.

A significant part of who I was, so I thought, as a person was linked to my identity at work. My life choices and lifestyle helped me to create independence and freedom. I could not easily begin to see where my life was headed after July 17th. Before I realized it, I began to sink into a severe depression.

The life I had become accustomed to, the person I once was months prior, and the career I spent over a decade building to prove every negative thing I heard as a child wrong were gone. I began walking around as a shell of myself.

I was no longer me. I had become this other person that people couldn't easily recognize. I would laugh and smile around my friends and family. I wanted them to think that I was okay. I didn't want them to have to worry about me. I didn't want to burden them with my problems. I hid behind my mask. A device that was destroying me.

If I told people my thoughts or feelings, I knew they wouldn't be able to handle it. The select few that I did tell would say, "Oh, well, everything happens for a reason. God has a plan."

I knew there was truth to their words. I had not forgotten my experience in the hospital. I just wasn't in a place to receive it. Remember you will also come across others who are not in a place to receive, extend grace to them.

Thank God, I had some money saved because I had been a good steward of my finances. I was and am frugal. Working with budgets for the past ten-plus years definitely paid off personally. God will prepare you for a season you have no idea is even coming.

In 2016, I relocated from Highlands, Indiana. I was fortunate to find a job in Tallahassee. Tallahassee gave me an opportunity of a lifetime. I always prayed for God to show me how to be a good steward of my blessings. This has always been a core prayer. God gave me my past difficulties so that my future prayers would serve me. Read again: I said, "God gave me my past difficulties so that my future prayers would serve me." The job changed my life and perspective on so many levels. I know what it is like to have nothing, so when I gained access to more resources, I prayed for guidance. Having only one income, I had to be frugal. I wanted to make sure I never knew another hungry night. The hunger and poverty I experienced in college drove me to be financially disciplined. God knew this time would come, and I see now that every situation before was to prepare me for this next phase of my journey.

A few months after being laid off, my depression consumed me. I would take a shower, lay naked in bed, and just stay there. Days would go by. I would just sleep for days. It was a tough period for me because I didn't know if I was coming or going. My life was at a standstill.

Before the layoff, I began seeing a therapist. To make matters worse, I was already off-balanced from a hostile work environment that was like an abusive relationship, according to my therapist. My soul and mind were in a million pieces. As a black woman, I felt as if I wasn't allowed to hurt. I wasn't allowed to show pain or fear, and I was always supposed to have all the answers. Therapy became a place where I didn't have to have the answers. I could cry, be transparent, and be vulnerable without the fear of judgment. With the help of therapy, the seed that God planted in me from my encounter with the pastor deepened my relationship with God. I was able to begin to see the light at the end of the tunnel. That light was a reflection of my purpose in searching for me.

Chapter Two

Growing Up In Pain

I was abused as a child. I was mentally, physically, and emotionally abused. I remember how my heart raced when I ran away from home at fifteen, the pounding in my ears. I remember my sweaty palms as I climbed over the fence, praying that I wouldn't fall and make any sound that would alert my mother. I remember the deep feeling of fear of the darkness I was staring at as I ran and the darkness in my soul.

There were not very many kind words exchanged in our household. We never ate dinner as a family at the dinner table. Holidays and birthdays were no special event. The air in our home was thick with tension all the time. I was never enough. Nothing I did was ever good enough; nothing I did ever deserved love.

I remember being told by my stepdad that I wasn't his child. We were on a fishing trip, and my mom and stepdad had just gotten married. I was so excited to finally have a dad. I had never met my biological father. He is now dead. Benjamin Carl Marbury died from a brain aneurysm at 41 years old. I will never have the answers my heart desperately needs. I am still making peace with this fact. I now understand that my stepdad was scared and did not know how to process going from being a single man to now a married man with a child. Yes, it was wrong for him to treat me this way, but he has shown me so much love and support in my adult life. He is my dad that stepped up. I am now a Daddy's girl. But that is a story for another time.

I remember in seventh grade we received our first report cards, I had all As and one B. I knew my mother was going to kill me. As the warm salty tears touched my lips, my classmates began to make fun of me. They did not understand what I was about to go home to. How could they? Some of their parents would have jumped over the moon if their kids had these same grades. My mother always made me feel that if I did not make a perfect score, I didn't do my best. I wasn't working hard enough, and for this, I would pay. I would pay with push-ups, beatings, abnormal chores, and harsh words. "I hate you. You make my stomach turn, and the only connection we have is that I gave birth to you." These words were said to a daughter by her own mother. Well, this scarred me so deeply that I still struggle with the by-product of this scar on my heart today.

I remember being sent to Boot Camp where my mom worked because I had lost my virginity. My mom read my diary and almost choked me to death. She might have succeeded if my stepdad had not pulled her off me. I remember the look in my mother's eyes as she lay on top of me and watched me struggle for air. Her eyes were dark and did not look human. I have never been able to completely run away from this image; it haunts me.

The school was always my happy place, and books were my best friends. This was also the only social time I had. I was not allowed to go to school dances or participate in after-school activities. After school, I always had to sprint home as I only had fifteen minutes from the second the bell rang to get home. If I was one minute late,

… that was my ass. Literally.

On weekends, I had to wake up at 5:00 am to complete my chores. I had to be done by 10:00 am. This included all laundry, the entire house from top to bottom, and mowing the backyard. I was always in a heightened state of mind, with my adrenaline always rushing from the fear of what the day's beating would hold. Sometimes, it was a Lysol can thrown at my face, causing my nose to bleed. As the blood dripped to the floor, my mother would say, "That's what you get from blowing your nose so hard." *Now, let's pause for a second. I have a big nose, and I have to blow it to unclog it, so I always made a trumpet sound when I blew my nose. It's funny now, but it wasn't funny then.* Other times, I would be beaten with an extension cord while standing on one leg naked.

As I have grown into my adulthood, I began hiding the ugly parts of my story in deep parts of my mind. My abandonment issues began to show up in my life. An unknown yet familiar feeling began consuming me during my depressive state. It caused me to lose sleep, and lack energy, and my appetite was completely off-kilter. I either didn't eat at all or I over-ate everything. I began thinking about my relationship with my mother. Growing up, I recall seeking my mother's love and affection. I was desperate for it. No matter how hard I tried to get her to love me, she just couldn't. The emotional abuse I suffered is similar to how I feel now. I strongly feel as though my childhood was stolen from me.

With all of these childhood memories circling in my mind and facing the fact that a job I had given so much to lay me off. I became the devil's playground. I was in a mental and spiritual warfare that had a perfect platform. I started having thoughts, like "I'm a failure," or "I'm not worthy." "I don't deserve to live." I felt lost. I would just lay in bed on my phone getting lost in the social media rabbit hole.

The best release I had was when I was in therapy. Therapy was the only place I could really be myself.

At this time, I was embarrassed to share that I was in therapy and the reasons I needed to be in therapy to begin with. I've always been perceived as the one that is put together. People have high expectations of me. I was terrified of what they would think of me if I showed vulnerability.

One thing for certain, if it hadn't been for the Lord keeping my mind stable, I wouldn't have made it through. One of the lessons that 2020 made me realize was that even when you barely have a grip on life, on wanting to live, God is holding you, even when you are crying blood and even when you are in the pit of darkness. I felt that the pandemic destroyed me. It made me lose my sense of purpose. God's love was the light that pierced through the darkest of my days.

Chapter Three

Identity

I AM A BLACK AMERICAN WOMAN.

Being black in America carries its own weight and burden, for men and women. In my experience as a black woman, I've come to normalize working hard to be accepted in most spaces. While in my previous work position, I had to carry the torch of being more responsible than my peers. As black women, we adapt to fear in different environments out of not being taken seriously. Gaining respect from others as a Black woman is quite the challenge of a lifetime. You have to understand early on as a black woman that you'll have to work twice as hard in order to establish at least half of a decent quality of life. We unknowingly carry the harsh reality of having to prove our worth to humanity daily. Being an American comes with its own negative perceptions in our country. Other cultures oftentimes associate black women as being uncultured, lazy, and hard to work with in different environments. The bizarre part of it all is that everyone loves the black culture, not black people.

As I come into more understanding as a black woman, I realize we come from a beautiful heritage. We've come a long way to make progress and create opportunities for ourselves. We no longer have to work within unhealthy environments that don't support our professional well-being. We've come so far to discuss how mental health affects our communities and families openly and publicly. I want people to know that being a black woman is not all about the perception of black girl magic or living a fast life. Being a black woman is not just about being strong for everyone else and being empty on the inside. Being a black woman is about rising up and living up to your expectations, prioritizing your health, supporting your family, pursuing your passion, and living under the word of God. Black women are not just superheroes, the other woman, the side chick, or the supportive best friend in your life. Black women deserve to be loved, protected, respected, and valued in every capacity of their lives.

On a personal and spiritual level, I declare that as a black woman, I am a warrior. As a black woman, I can give, start a business, run for political office, star in a movie, or become an all-star athlete. There are no limits to who we are as black women.

Chapter Four

Challenges

2020 WAS TRULY ONE FOR THE HISTORY BOOKS.

Who would have ever thought that there would be a racial uprising in the middle of a pandemic? The pandemic pushed all of us into unfamiliar territories. Many people lost their businesses or jobs. Schools were shut down. Curfews were implemented across the country, and racial tension rose.

The pandemic really pushed us all into a box. It forced many of us to face our darkest fears and the ugly parts of ourselves. Many of us were not mentally or spiritually prepared to handle life during a global pandemic.

The gruesome death of George Floyd's murder added fuel to the fire. The video sparked something in all of us that called us all to action. We had all reached our breaking point. We demanded change because it was too much to ignore. On a personal note, I suffered in silence in many ways. I felt like a prisoner in my mind, body, and home very often. My depression and lack of motivation started to reflect in my appearance. I started to put on more weight as the days turned into weeks and weeks into months. I was never 100 % myself during the pandemic.

What was happening outside of my home only further triggered me into a downward spiral. It was hard for me to digest it all on my own. I was in a constant state of anxiety and frustration. I needed to find relief.

Let's break down 2020.

First the pandemic.

The coronavirus was first detected in Wuhan, China, in late 2019, and the first cases made their way to the United States in JanuaryShutdownst downs officially began in March. As for me, I was considered an essential worker within my industry. I was thrown into the midst of all the chaos. It was quite strange to be open for business when the country/world was filled with a lot of uncertainty. Before we all could blink an eye, everything around us began to shut down. It began with supply chain disruptions, government closures, and corporate layoffs. Every industry was affected, including the entertainment industry.

The things that we all enjoyed doing in our leisure time were no longer available. Perhaps, the biggest conflict of all was the mandate to wear a mask daily. You could not walk into a grocery store, post office, or restaurant without a mask.

It was madness on top of madness. There was so much misinformation flooding the airwaves and media that it would make your head spin. Everyone adjusted to the pandemic and mandate very differently. On one hand, the mask could prevent the spread of the virus. Yet, there were groups that were against the mask mandate. At the same time, the virus would continuously spread around the country.

At the peak of the pandemic, there was the video of George Floyd crying out for his mother. It broke millions of people's hearts around the world. It was the hardest thing to watch on social media and the news. Simultaneously, you have the Amy Cooper incident where a white woman made a false police report about a black man harassing her and her dog in central park. These events happening on the same day sparked national outrage and a revolution that was ultimately televised.

The black community was being attacked in multiple ways. The disproportionate effects of the virus, mass job loss, police brutality, and an uprising in crime caused the black community to push back. For the longest time, other cultures have stood back on the sidelines and watched black people demand justice. As a community, we are not unfamiliar with boycotting and rioting to get the attention needed for a problem. With the pandemic and social media, the issues facing the black community could not be ignored, and allies in the Asian community or across the globe pushed the issue to the forefront of America's doorstep.

Protests erupted all over the world. Businesses burned to the ground, and national guards along with police in riot guards were appointed to state lines. The world was watching and waiting for answers to disrupt the normalcy of black life in America.

***

Shortly after the release of the George Floyd video, more videos began to appear on the internet. One video that particularly stood out more than many others was the viral video of a black woman describing a racist encounter. The incident involved a woman on an elevator with mostly white men who refused to allow her to pass. A white woman occupied the same elevator. As the elevator came to the stop and doors opened to exit, the older white gentleman allowed the white woman to pass.

Once the black woman tried to pass through the crowded elevator, she was blocked with an umbrella. The white male passenger stated sternly, "Ladies first!"

Although there were other white men present in the elevator, they ignored the comment and exited the elevator. When I learned of this incident, it lit a fire inside of me. This black woman's experience was not uncommon or unfamiliar to me. Our history in this country when it comes to black women feeling unprotected or unsafe is one I know all too well. As black women, we are often mistreated in public, harassed, and assaulted by men. More often than not, people don't speak up or come to our defense. In many ways, it feels as if people believe black women are getting what they deserve in these situations.

I recognize this moment as something that as black women, we go through every day in this country. It's not fair. It's our reality. Although we can't demand for other people to step in and fight our battles for us, it's important for black women to feel valued and seen in any situation. These situations cannot continue to be ignored and rest on the shoulders of the black woman. We are not the victims and superheroes of our own story. We are stronger when we speak out against any injustice that happens to us. It begins there when we speak up and tell the world, "You're not going to treat me less than I deserve." "I am human." "I deserve to be respected and protected."

This is why our self-care looks so different from other women's. We have a long history in this country of silencing our suffering. We have learned through generations and centuries of mental trauma that have impacted our lives to this day.

As black women, when we declare that we are "reclaiming our time," it's not just for likes or validation. It's our declaration to the world that I will no longer push down my trauma and allow you to beat me with a stick.

As black women today, with the help of social media, we can now visualize and support our growth. We can champion each other to our goals and encourage each other to be transparent and vulnerable. Today, black women have created a number of our own self-care and self-help brands, black-centered content, and a multitude of online communities specifically for black women. This is why black women are the fastest-growing entrepreneurs in the US. In the words of Kendrick Lamar, "We gon' be alright."

Chapter Five

Mental Health Awareness

When it comes to mental health, I find that as black women, we have to extend grace to ourselves. For many black women, we don't allow ourselves to feel sad. We have to allow ourselves room to grow. That growth begins with looking within and doing the in-depth work to cleanse our souls, deprogram and reprogram. It begins with a willingness to improve certain aspects of our life. For many of us, we have to admit to ourselves that something in our lives needs more attention. It takes a hard look in the mirror and open dialogue with yourself to do the work.

As black women, we cannot be afraid to recalibrate and try a different approach to becoming our best selves. When it comes to our mental health as black women, we have been taught to compartmentalize our feelings. For the longest time, as black women, we have been groomed to be strong at all times. It's not okay to appear weak around your family, friends, or colleagues. You cannot fold under pressure. You have to rise above it all and be okay from day to day. The reality is that it does more damage to ignore yourself or pretend that everything is ok when it's not.

Many times, black women experience more depression, anxiety, and stress because they don't have an outlet. Unfortunately, our churches don't encourage us to seek counseling for mental health. It's taboo in the black community. You are more so encouraged to pray away the thoughts inside your head, and everything will work itself out. I strongly believe there is a time and place for prayer in our lives. However, when it comes to finding a safe place to open up without judgment, therapy can help.

For me, therapy has been a pivotal relationship for my growth and healing. When I'm in therapy, I feel safe enough to let my walls come down and be vulnerable. I don't have to pretend to be someone else or hide from my truth. In therapy, I am safe to let my guard down without judgment. During therapy, I realized that my thoughts could be released. It's a reassuring feeling to know that therapy has helped to provide me with the tools to navigate my way through life.

When it comes to discovering how you can obtain mental health in your life, it begins with setting realistic and attainable goals.

You can start by learning to be kind to yourself. When you start your day, give yourself words of encouragement. Acknowledge how beautiful you look and all the things you are grateful for. The words you speak to yourself are the most important conversations you'll have each and every day. You will forever battle within yourself. Your old self and old habits will always be around the corner waiting for you to slip up.

What are you putting inside your body? Most of us reach for a quick, fast, and hot meal when we're tired. You have to be conscious of the foods that you put in your body. Have discipline and self-control over the food you eat. You can have cookies and fried food in moderation. It's more important to eat a well-balanced meal that gives your body nourishment. You need to properly fuel your body. After all, your body is the only vessel you have on this earth. Protect and care for it.

Please be conscious of the words that come out of your mouth. Sometimes, we are often quick to respond to our life situations with negativity. Just as we are what we eat, we are also what we speak.

Implement the habit of speaking and responding positively to moments of difficulty in your life. More often than not, we speak harshly to ourselves and don't recognize. You know, like when someone compliments us, and instead of just saying thank you, we point out an imperfection to counteract that compliment. Subconsciously, we are telling ourselves we are not worthy.

It becomes strange when people recognize the negativity within us. No one likes to be called out, but you must master calling yourself out. You must learn to master yourself. This will be a never-ending journey. This will not be an assignment that has a due date, and then, you are done with the said assignment. You must accept the fact that the journey to true mastery is an ongoing project with no end.

We have to make a conscious effort to speak life into ourselves. We have many things to distract and destroy the way we feel about ourselves in this world. We don't need to be self-destructive. Learning to speak positively to yourself can be strange in the beginning. It will sound funny or uncomfortable, but the more you learn to adapt to this way of thinking, you will begin to normalize this behavior. It helps to pick up the bible and read encouraging scriptures at the start of your day, download apps with daily affirmations, tune into podcasts with positive messaging, or join a prayer circle at your church. Now, if all of that seems like too much, start with posting love notes on your bathroom mirror, by your coffee machine, or on your nightstand, so you see positive words when you first wake up.

One of the most life-changing exercises I use to date is my morning ritual. I keep a bottle of water by my bed at all times. When

I wake up, I don't just jump up and start my day. I give myself time. I sit on the edge of my bed, take deep breaths, and drink my bottle of water. While drinking my water, I thank God for another day of life. I gather my thoughts and make mental notes of my priorities. I always make my bed and spray a special lavender mist in my room. The last thing I do is massage my body. This is to promote circulation and relaxation before my day even starts. I am not a doctor, but I find that my anxiety is almost nonexistent when I am intentional about what I feed my senses at the start of my day. I encourage you to find a morning ritual that is sustainable for you. Work the day and don't let it work you!

Another part of therapy is being cognitive of the consistency that you allow yourself to fall in or out of in your life. Accountability plays a major role in therapy. When it comes to therapy, you'll need to identify and connect with a therapist that will hold you accountable for your growth. During therapy, you will receive exercises that you need to complete before and after therapy. Completing these exercises is critical to your therapeutic journey.

You have to have a clear understanding of what you want to get out of therapy and work towards that goal. When we talk about mental health, you must have a clear understanding of what it takes to have a healthy mindset and attitude about life.

I believe that when you have a clear perspective on how therapy can help you heal from your past and prepare you for your future, you will understand why now more than ever, more people are speaking out about their need for mental health.

When I look back on all that I went through in 2020, I now recognize being laid off was a blessing in disguise. While I was going through my layoff and hostility in the workplace, I realized I had a lot of emotional stress from my childhood that was coming to the surface also.

With everything happening all at once, it scared me. It caused me to put my focus on the one thing I could control, which was my career. As I have progressed through my career and obtained more skills that can transfer to different industries, it encouraged me to jump back into the workforce after my layoff.

I may not have made as much money as I was making before, but I was financially prepared. I knew that starting over in a different industry would be hard. But I prayed, did my research, and came up with a game plan. God blessed me. He made sure that I didn't go hungry. I may not have had everything I wanted, but I had all I needed. During the pandemic, I was able to obtain the first of many licenses I knew I would need for my five-year plan—a Life and Annuity Insurance license. I learned how to make connections with the right people to grow my business.

I began helping families establish financial freedom. As I began to grow with my new industry, I was still making much less than I was accustomed to. I often made less, a lot less than what my monthly bills added up to be. Thus, my perspective on maintaining my financial stability came into question. Being financially unstable began to trigger my mental peace. I began to ask myself if I could actually make it during the pandemic.

I had to make up my mind about where I wanted to be in five to ten years. I needed to figure out how I would make it from point A to point B. I decided to be intentional about my financial decisions and take steps towards a better lifestyle.

I was no fool; I also knew that what I was gaining would provide me the leverage of experience for a future position. My compensation would not come instantaneously. I kept reminding myself to stick to the plan and trust the process. With my prayer, action, and faith, there was no way I could fail. I might get knocked down from time to time and have to redirect my efforts, but if I didn't stop, my progress would continue.

I continued to work long hours, being a manager at a local restaurant by night and working from home during the day while still managing my mental and financial health. My spiritual health has helped empower me to take bold steps toward my future. I began making conscious decisions to read scriptures—maybe not as much as I should, but more than I used too. I extended grace to myself and encouraged myself to keep going. Losing focus is a part of the process of you growing. As you learn to shift forward and let go of old habits, you will lose momentum. The important thing to understand is that there is always a chance for you to get back up. No matter how many times you get knocked down during the battles of life and the war you face every day within yourself. If you can look up, you can get back up and try again and again. You don't stop trying ever! Got it?

Take a step back and allow yourself the opportunity to recharge and reevaluate your life choices. Whether you make a few mistakes along the way, you'll become stronger the longer you stay committed to the process. Sometimes, it's a constant battle that you will have to learn to adjust too.

Be ready. You will face many ups and downs. There is no cheat code, and you can't skip hard work. How you choose to respond to adversity is all that matters. Be aware and accept that you cannot control the hand that life has dealt you. You can only control how you play your hand.

When we talk about mental growth, it's important to realize that NOT being okay is okay. You have to approach life with the clear understanding that you can set forth mechanisms in your life that allow you to get better each and every day. One specific mechanism

I would like to share with you is my state of mind when I take a shower. Don't get weird with me, hear me out.

A technique I learned from one of my therapy sessions has helped me begin my day with balance. When I get in the shower in the morning, I pay attention to any tension in my body. Is my heart racing? Is there tension in my shoulders? Is my breathing abnormal? I mentally focus on those areas and link the feeling of water running over me. Washing away the pain, sadness, insecurities, and all negative thoughts. As the warm water flows down my body and into the shower drain, I picture myself being washed clean of all negative thoughts. I literally watch them flow down the drain. When I step out of my shower, I feel lighter. You can choose to condition your mind to take care of yourself.

When you look at things from an optimistic standpoint versus a pessimistic standpoint, you'll understand that you're in a powerful position to the outcome of your destiny. I'm a believer in "What you speak comes back to you". If you speak positive things, positive things come back to you. If you always speak negatively, you will cotinine to feel negative about the place you are in your journey.

There are life lessons that are going to come back to you in different ways. Be prepared for these lessons to continue to repeat until you have gathered the tools you need for the next phase in your journey. Sometimes, it will be in the shape of love, friendships, relationships, or work. As human beings, we have a way of gravitating toward the energy we put out in the world. If you need help, keeping balance or keeping away from negativity. Don't be afraid to ask for help when you need it. Asking for help does not make you weak. Asking for help when you need it is wise. Don't be afraid to utilize the resources you have and don't be afraid to go find them either.

We have to be conscious of what we say to ourselves and others.

As black women, we have to put up with too much to not ask for help. I know, at times, I hate to feel like I'm being vulnerable with others. I struggle with feeling judged by others. It's a constant challenge for me to get out of my head and open up to other people. As black women, we have to get to a point where our mental health is more important than how somebody else feels about us. My grandfather always tells me, "It doesn't matter what other people think about you. They better worry about what you think about them." You have the power to control your paradigm of how you see the world and vice versa.

That's when your real strength and muscle builds. When you realize what God realizes about you, you become unstoppable. When you face so much hurt in your lifetime, you become a warrior in the game. When life-changing situations occur in your life, you will be prepared to handle them because you have built your muscle.

The best thing that you can do for yourself is to start to prepare for the opportunity you are praying for. Remember that preparation makes room for opportunity. After all, what good is the stage if your act is not ready? Start by taking classes, and courses online, and get certifications and licensing in your industry. Make yourself marketable and learn to pursue things that don't give you instant gratification. Permit yourself to prepare for the future you deserve. When you begin working towards the life you want, life will begin to reward your hard work. Many doors will begin to become unlocked for you. Things will begin to happen for you, not when you want them to, but right on time. Be consistent and intentional.

Here are a few tips that I picked up on improving your physical health. I am no guru. I just pray this helps you:

Everything Begins With Your Mindset

What are you feeding your mind daily? Your mindset can influence your thoughts, habits, and actions. Oftentimes, we ingest negative influences into our subconscious that we adopt into our routine. Our environments also contribute to poor health choices. The nearest health food store may be outside of your neighborhood. Thus, you may settle for fast food. Consider the option of making a healthy meal at home. Also, consider the savings to your budget when you cook your own meals. If you add up the money you spend on food that is convenient versus what you would spend if you planned ahead, you would find room in your budget to save more or invest the difference in another area of your budget. Simple tactics like this done over and over can make monumental differences in your financial health. The decision is up to you. A mind is like a sponge. It will absorb everything within its pathway. Pinpoint your triggers in a daily journal weekly. This will reveal to you your state of mind at the time you chose to eat poorly. You have the power to change your mind at any point. You must be willing and receptive to receiving information that will help get you on the right track.

Small Steps Lead To Big Rewards

Many people start their weight loss journey with great ambitions in mind. Most of us want rapid weight loss within months. We live in a fast-paced, instant gratification, and an easily accessible fix-it world where your problems may be resolved in minutes, not months. Our bodies are not equipped to go through drastic changes overnight. Same as we gain weight over a while, we must consider a steady well-balanced weight. Walking daily for thirty minutes or eating a well-balanced breakfast will help develop healthier habits. You build from there. I find it helpful to do small personal challenges. Start with committing to five days of drinking a gallon of water a day and eating a salad for lunch. The completion of personal challenges will help you to gain confidence. You will enjoy the feeling of accomplishment. Slowly add more time and goals to your personal challenges. Before you know it, the momentum will pick up if you stay consistent. It's important to acknowledge and reward yourself for your small wins along the journey to keep you motivated.

Nutrients To Boost Your Health

Growing up, our parents would always suggest we eat our veggies and take a vitamin before bed. Nowadays, we supplement our meals with instant drinks or veggie smoothies. Our parents were right. A standard serving of vegetables is 75g, which is equivalent to 1 medium tomato or one cup of green leafy salad. How do you ensure you get your daily serving of vegetables? Meal prep. Meal prepping for the week ahead is instrumental to a well-balanced diet and lifestyle. Meal prep will only require a few hours of your time each week. If you're an on-the-go person, you can grab a prepped meal from the fridge to fuel your body. You're less likely to overindulge in snacks or fast food when your tummy is full.

Get Active During The Day

Exercise is possibly one of the least favorite activities of most people. Between the gym environment being intimidating and the unfriendly outdoors, it can be challenging to find the perfect way to get your body moving. Although you can't control the elements, other people, or facilities, you can get up and move your body. According to the Mayo Clinic, exercise can help increase your mood, reduce stress, and promote a better night's rest. Getting your body accustomed to moving regularly is not easy or comfortable but focus more on your goals than your feelings on this one. Change is rarely comfortable. It's necessary for a longer and more rewarding healthy life.

Adopting A Positive Outlook On Life

The previous year was filled with more trauma and turmoil than anyone could have possibly imagined. Our normal coping methods have been restricted to the essentials of our homes. It's easier to lose hope than keep a positive attitude year-round. As mentioned previously, our mindsets are key indicators of whether we are doing well or struggling with our life choices. The conversations that we have with ourselves and others may be different. Just as your physical health is important, don't neglect your mental health. A few ways to see the good throughout your day are through podcasts, books, and meditational apps. You have resources at your fingertips that will help promote your mental wellness daily. You are on your phone anyway. Make it count!

You're Not Perfect, And That's Ok

Lastly, it took me a while to completely understand that life is a journey. Along the journey of self-healing and discovery, you're going to make some mistakes. Those mistakes are not permanent. Every obstacle is not a test of your endurance, it's a test of faith. Your setbacks and delays are meant to pressure you into diving deeper into yourself. You'll need to learn how to unravel all of the layers of the misconceptions of whom the world told you to be. Empower and encourage yourself to become the person you have always imagined. You'll never be perfect. You are a continuous work in progress. Cut yourself some slack and keep going until you reach your destination. This journey belongs to you.

Chapter Six

Dealing with Trauma

When we begin to discuss trauma, most people begin to run away from the issue. Our trauma lives on in our bodies. Although our minds may not be able to recall every detail of the experience when we begin to explore our trauma as we begin to unpack the parts of our lives that make us question our value.

Trauma forces us to reveal the things about ourselves that we'd never speak of again. For many of us, our trauma has left us wounded and scarred for life. As much as we would like to run away from our trauma, it follows us throughout our lives.

At some point, we must face our trauma and begin the healing process.

Dealing with trauma is more detailed than talking about your childhood. Everything begins with understanding that the trauma you experienced was not your fault. People who experience trauma blame themselves for not being in the right place. Not speaking up for themselves. Not knowing how to prevent what happened to them from happening in the first place.

Although you don't have any control over the past, you are not to blame for what happened. Unfortunately, in this life, bad things happen to us. The first step in dealing with our trauma is to acknowledge the hurt and pain. Be honest with yourself and stop running away from the pain. The pain may have numbed your heart from allowing other people to come into your life. You may consider yourself unlovable because you sabotage your relationships with people. These are all symptoms of living a life with unchecked trauma.

There are people in the world who have lived through trauma and have thriving lives. That can be you too.

Examine where you are in your life today. Are there areas of your life that you have ignored because of your trauma? Do you feel anxiety about changing your life?

If you answered yes, understand that you are not alone. There is hope on the other side of your life experience.

What is trauma?

According to Newsinhealth.gov, "Most people associate post-traumatic stress symptoms with veterans and combat situations," says Dr. Amit Etkin, an NIH-funded mental health expert at Stanford University. "However, all sorts of trauma happen during one's life that can lead to post-traumatic stress disorder and post-traumatic stress disorder-like symptoms." (https://newsinhealth.nih.gov/2018/06/dealing-trauma)

Consider the traumas that occur in our childhood. When we think of our childhood, we have to look at the relationships that were inside the home. Were your parents loving and supportive or combative and anxious towards each other? For many of us, our parents were unmarried and unprepared to raise a family. Some of us grew up knowing the fact that money was a necessity. However, money caused strife and tension between your parents. Money was not in surplus. You may have had to go without food or utilities for a while. Think about it.

That's considered to be a traumatic event.

According to the National Center for Post-Traumatic Stress Disorder, "About 7 or 8 out of every 100 people will experience PTSD at some point in their lives." (https://newsinhealth.nih.gov/2018/06/dealing-trauma)

When we don't understand trauma, we don't know how to treat those in our lives who are experiencing PTSD. We assume that those who have been impacted are hiding from us or rather be left alone. PTSD is not something that you can work through with a glass of wine or a vacation. You have to be patient and mindful of the impact that trauma may have on the mind and behaviors of others.

Your trauma is not who you are. It's an event that occurred at a particular time in your life. Where you are in your life today is a direct reflection of your choices and decisions. You've made a series of choices that have allowed you to improve your life on your terms. When you think of your trauma, you don't have to wear it as a badge or hide in plain sight. Your trauma does not have to rule your life. Just as you have made difficult decisions to create a better life, you can stand in the trauma and not drown. You can choose to heal on your terms.

Most people believe that because of their trauma, they will never know love or happiness. It's not true. When you consider high-profile people like Tyler Perry, who talks openly about his molestation, you would think that he would never want to speak in public again. The shame and burden of carrying the secret of his pain could have buried him. Instead, Tyler Perry should be an example that although bad things happen to good people, we don't have to allow negative traumas to change our lives forever.

Through his transparency, Tyler has helped more people live courageous and bold lives.

Now, it's your turn.

Although you may have learned how to cope with the pain by not talking about it, or pretending it never happened has held you together for so long, you must understand that your current coping mechanism will only take you so far.

The coping mechanism you developed to protect yourself may be the very tool that you allow to destroy you. Don't let your fear put you in a position to self-sabotage. The same tools you needed to survive are not the same tools you will need to thrive. You can't use a hammer on a screw. You can and most likely, will do more harm with brute force than the correct tactic in the right situation. Learn emotional intelligence. Know the importance of pausing and thinking before you speak. Don't react, respond on and in your purpose.

Deal with what happened to you. Don't run or hide from it. Examine how you feel. Take note of the smells, sounds, and words that trigger your trauma. Pay attention to how your body feels. Is your chest tight? Do your hands sweat? Do you begin to lose track of your thoughts? Do you get angry and not understand why? Learn yourself and be cognitive when and why your moods shift.

Don't run from your thoughts. There is no drug or person that can make what happened to you go away. Know that you are not defined by what has happened to you in your life. Rather how you respond and what you have let it turn you into. Have you let your pain make you bitter and pessimistic? Or have you let your pain fuel you to be a help or aid that you wish you had?

When you are ready to deal with your trauma, seek the advice and support of your trusted family. You will need to be around people that you love and trust. Make sure that you feel safe in a space where you're not judged or ridiculed. With the right support and guidance, your trauma will no longer be something you have to deal with alone.

Chapter Seven

Live in Intention

When COVID-19 hit home with a lot of deaths, it rocked us to the core. We watched as young babies, the elderly, and spouses die unexpectedly from contracting the virus. As human beings, we have an understanding that mortality is fragile. COVID forced us to look at the fragile state of our mortality. COVID-19 helped to expose that to the world. Many people experienced a lot of mental grief. There was a lot of mental stress across the world.

For me, every day seemed like there was a family member or a loved one that was either in the hospital, passing away unexpectedly, or in critical condition on a ventilator due to COVID-19. The pandemic forced us to deal with death constantly. Every ethnic group suffered from the mental strain and impact of COVID. Not many people discuss the lack of comfort and mental strain that comes with the aftermath of COVID. Many people experience a mental state of numbness. As we began to digest the news reports and read the timelines of our social media friends, we all incoherently became desensitized to the negative information.

When we become so consumed with living or dying daily, our perspectives shift into a state of fear and panic. We are living in a constant state of worrying and mental suffrage. With all that occurred in 2020, it's important to realize that we are all born to die. We were not created to live for all eternity.

We were born to live, and then, we will die in order to complete that cycle. No matter if death comes in the form of COVID-19 or other issues related to the pandemic. Mental health is realizing the truth in a conscious state of being. The truth of the matter is, you were born to live your life purposefully. Despite the challenges and situations, you're going to move through life with intention in order to complete the circle of life path. Part of mental growth is realizing that in between living and dying. You have an opportunity to live. Live each day with intention. Live each day with purpose. Live each day with the mentality of becoming a better you. Don't compare yourself to another person's story. Live each day to be the best you that you can be. The only competition that you should put yourself in is to become better than you were yesterday. As I go through these different chapters of my own journey, I, too, have realized that the most important part between living and dying is the people that I touch in my life. I have cultivated long-term friendships, and acquaintances at work, and met beautiful souls in the grocery store or post office.

How do you live with intention? I start by waking up every day with gratitude in my heart. Every morning I say out loud, "I thank you Jesus for allowing me to live another day. Thank you, Lord, for another chance to get life right." It all starts with you.

Begin each day by asking yourself, "What do you want to accomplish today? How do you want to make an impact in the world? How do you want to feel at the end of each day?"

When you can be truthful about your intentions, you will see the world differently. Along the way, it's important to treat your body well physically. Start with taking a walk or stretching your joints. Recite positive affirmations to yourself. Uplift other people in your life with words of encouragement and acknowledgment. This genuine behavior will cause the right people to gravitate to you. When you receive negative information, don't hold on to it in your spirit. Release it back where it came from and rest in the true power of faith.

As you began to take more conscious steps into loving and trusting yourself, your identity will change. You might not easily recognize yourself. Your new life will cost you your old one. Expect an expensive bill. Don't bargain with yourself. Stick to the plan. Pay yourself what you owe every single day. These daily deposits will have a high return on your investment.

You'll be able to capture yourself from being a pessimistic person to an optimistic person. As you begin to shed old habits and transform your mind, you allow healing to occur in your life. You will begin to heal as you allow yourself to go through the cleansing of your heart. Your mental space will not feel overloaded and crammed with things that distract you from your purpose. You will begin to expand with the fruitfulness of being happy and living in a state of joy.

Within the last year, I have made some significant changes in my life. Starting with the time of day I go to bed. I've learned that I need at least seven hours of sleep to function properly. I start my day with a well-balanced meal for breakfast. I have started taking nutritious foods to lunch that will help keep me alert and focused. I am intentional when it comes to drinking water periodically.

Each task helps contribute to the person I want to become in the future. I'm no longer going with the flow of things or settling for a small piece of what I deserve. I'm intentionally creating the life I desire and deserve with my actions.

On my less-than-perfect days, I don't beat myself up. I offer myself grace as God offers us grace and mercy. I'm a work in progress, just like you. We owe it to ourselves to not fight our progress. If you recognize that you're doing the best that you can, honor that.

The goal is progress, not perfection. There may be some days when you fall short, don't quit. I know life gets hard and throws you a few curve balls occasionally. Even when I face difficult moments, I realize that there are lessons and opportunities for me to grow.

Mental health and spiritual health are about becoming a better person than you were yesterday. You are your biggest competition. The only competitor that you should see is yourself. I want to be better than I was yesterday and tomorrow. My goal is to be better than I am today. I believe that when we speak about mental and spiritual growth, it's important that we set forth boundaries and limitations. When we are mindful of how we choose to respond to life or people, we honor ourselves. We take back the power to allow others to destroy us with words and actions. We stand in our truth and protect our peace with boundaries. We become stronger the more we have a distinctive difference in what we will allow into our lives.

Learning to establish healthy boundaries has helped me to manage my anxiety. I give myself room to be present and learn within the moment. I extend grace to myself and others. Don't beat yourself up because you don't complete 100% of your tasks. Make a digital note on your phone and make those missed tasks a priority the next day.

We have to learn to feed ourselves, for where we see ourselves. What do I mean? Every morning, I tune in to inspirational messages versus hip-hop music. I'm intentionally feeding my body, mind, and spirit messages of hope and encouragement. I am aware that there are people who have been where I am, and they are striving to get out of difficult situations. My message is to get in alignment with the things that uplift your spirit. We have many distractions in our world from the news, social media, work, friends, and more. It can be hard to see the sunshine with rain and distraction in your eyes.

Don't lose hope. Find something in your life that allows you to feel free and at peace. For some of us, that could be writing, painting, dancing, singing, or rebuilding homes. Whatever that special thing is that brings you joy, do it often. You deserve the peace and happiness you freely give away to others.

Chapter Eight

Become Spiritually Aware

I wake up every morning now, and I thank God. I thank God for allowing me to wake up to see a new day. How you choose to start your day sets the tone for the entire day. I set aside the first twenty minutes of my day in shifting my energy into a positive space. Earlier, I shared my morning ritual with you, and again, I encourage you to find one that works for you and stick with it. Working out has helped me achieve mental and spiritual growth. There are lessons that the gym and working out will teach you. Linking physical and mental discipline will turn you into a new creature. This space will water your personal growth and teach you mental and spiritual fortitude. Results seen from your hard work and consistency will give you confidence in your abilities. Suddenly, obstacles that use to seem so big or out of reach will become attainable. When I began to move my body and focus my mind on the goodness of God, I felt most alive. I honor God in my most vulnerable and sacred moments because He deserves it. I thank God for my body, the mobility of my limbs, and the breath in my lungs. I am in a state of gratitude and appreciation.

I thank God for the blessings He has given me, for my loved ones, and for divine connections. My spiritual growth has allowed me to take steps of courage and faith where I once resided in the depths of despair and mental anguish. I have found clarity and peace in knowing that I am a child of God, and He loves me. He wants the best for me. He protects and provides for me. I would be nothing without his love, grace, and mercy.

Throughout my life journey, I have had to sacrifice many things to obtain peace today. I am more spiritually at peace than ever before in my life. For the first time, I am falling in love with myself. I encourage you to be willing to let go and allow spiritual healing to occur in your life. I pray you learn to fall in love with yourself first! When you are on the journey of becoming spiritually self-aware, you have to be prepared to let go. Let go of the many distractions that take you away from your purpose. Sometimes, a distraction can be a loved one or a budding relationship. It is important to gain control over your emotions so that how feel does not blind you to what is in front of you. We ignore the red flags as big as day because our ability to see them has been compromised. Our friends can distract us from our full potential too. Remember, it is ok and necessary to block out the outside world and unplug for a while. Take intentional time to focus. Put your phone on silent, stay off social media, and observe how much more you get done in a day. Anything that is taking you away from your purpose or clouding your judgment is a distraction. Love yourself enough to be honest with what your next steps should be. You already know what you need to do deep down, so do it!

In most cases, people attempt to pull back from their distractions by fasting. When people hear the word "fast," they think it's about a diet or deprivation. That's not quite true. Being able to fast means that you deprive yourself of things that give you pleasure in order to gain clarity and guidance toward a goal. For example, most mornings, I used to open my eyes and reach for my cell phone. I needed to check my Facebook notifications. I would become so distracted by social media that I would be late for work. When I began to fast from social media, I was able to become more productive in the mornings. We have to begin to spiritually transform our mindsets.

When it comes to spiritual growth, you need to put yourself in a state of fasting. Don't get on social media every day. Create a daily habit that will help bring you mental clarity and peace daily. It could be reading a book on self-development or meditation. Once you begin to consciously eliminate your distractions, you will become more productive.

Another way that can help you become more spiritually aware is to stop gossiping. More often than not, we spend a lot of time on the phone discussing our life problems with people who can't help us. Most people just want to know how you're doing and if they're doing better than you. You give people access to your life by sharing private information. The same goes for when people call you to vent or spill the tea about other people. How does this information benefit you? Does it help you achieve your goals? Does it bring you peace and understanding about life? Probably not.

The truth of the matter is that gossiping only leads to more gossiping. It just helps the other person accomplish their goal of spreading bad news. None of us can use more bad news. When people call you to gossip, tell them you don't have the time. You're not lying or being mean. You're protecting your peace. Don't allow others to disrupt you from going after what you want in life. Whether it's studying for the bar exam or renewing your business license, stay focused.

You have the power in your tongue to speak what you want to accomplish in your life. Stop allowing other people's dilemmas and obstacles to become your problem. You can love people and show compassion for their situation, but you can't give up or stop pursuing your goals because of every emergency happening in their lives. When we begin to believe in the things we say to ourselves, we don't allow others to come in and destroy our beliefs. You have to become stubborn about chasing the life of your dreams. You have to become hungry. Sometimes, you even have to be on a rampage to meet the best version of yourself. You're never too old or too young to make better life decisions.

Instead of telling yourself that you don't have time to accomplish your goal, change the deadline and continue to work towards the goal. You have to be willing to sacrifice a little to gain a lot. For many of us, the hardest sacrifice is being available to our friends and family. People will need you to come to this event or support this cause. The truth of the matter is you'll have to decline some of the invitations. When you're on the road to creating a new path for yourself, you don't have a lot of free time to socialize or hang out as much. You're preparing yourself for something much greater in life, and not everyone will understand that.

When you want spiritual growth to occur in your life, you will need people around you that will support your path. Many of us walk through life and never discover our purpose. Why? We don't know ourselves or God. We spend a lot of time intentionally distracting ourselves with worldly things too often. Many of us don't spend enough time reading the scripture. Often, we neglect our opportunities to connect with positive or like-minded individuals. Instead, we entertain conversations that have nothing to do with our purpose or goals.

Whom we invite our lives says a lot about us and the direction we're headed. Some of us are headed for self-destruction, and the people in our lives are bystanders. It may be hard or challenging, in the beginning, to break away from what you've always known. But the ultimate sacrifice is the time it takes to correct our wrongs. Choose people that inspire you to go after what you want in life. Choose people that will fuel your dreams, not your fears. Choose people that will motivate you when you can't motivate yourself.

Ask yourself this question before you engage in a certain topic with someone: is this person capable of absorbing the information that I have to give? Does their mindset allow them to absorb this information or are they not capable?

That doesn't mean they're any less of a person. That just means you prepare yourself to speak to the audience in front of you. Know your audience, whether it's one person or a group of people. Know whom you're talking to.

Protect your peace. What does that mean? Protecting your peace means you are becoming wiser in knowing when to hold your tongue and speak your thoughts. Sometimes, everything that is said to you does not require a response. You'll be surprised how strong and how impactful silence can truly be. If you are angry, be silent. If you're not sure, be silent. If you need time to research and think about a topic, be silent. When you learn to control yourself, you can better control the outcome.

Understand that growth is not meant to be comfortable, get comfortable out of your head. When you're comfortable, it will kill your momentum to grow. Stepping outside of your comfort zone is easier said than done. For many of us, we have become stuck in a pattern of doing what feels good or easy. When you want better for yourself, you have to be willing to step outside of your comfort zone. Our comfort zone can make us feel as if we have it all figured out. Or that this is all that life has to offer, so why should we want to pursue better? Every person that is successful today has to step outside of their comfort zone. If you refuse to grow, life will only challenge you with difficult circumstances. You will be forced into a corner with no options.

Life gives us opportunities to grow in many different ways. Sometimes, we may not be ready when the opportunity appears. I encourage you to step out on faith and go after what you want. Don't become complacent in life. You must always keep your eyes open and focused on your goals. Sometimes, you can look around, and life will have passed you by. Don't get caught in the trap of working all your life then you don't enjoy the simple things. The most important things in life are free. Love of family, love of self, and love of community are all free and available to you. Many people fail to accomplish their dreams out of fear of failure. Failure will look different to many people. You might consider yourself a failure if you had to get your G.E.D. instead of your diploma. You might consider yourself a failure if you didn't finish school or go to college. I've learned through many trials and tribulations that failure is not permanent or final. Failure is an attempt to attain a goal, with no success. You have the opportunity to try again and again. Just because you didn't accomplish what you set out in the beginning and did not achieve it. Don't allow failure to define who you are as a person. We tie our failures to our identity too often. Our identity is not defined by our accomplishments. When set out to accomplish a task or goal, we put a lot of effort and intention behind it. Thus, when we don't accomplish it, it hurts our ego. Although the failure or loss may sting for a little bit, no one ever stops you from trying again.

We walk away from our goals too often because we feel embarrassed. There is no need to feel embarrassed by your failed attempts. Life gives us an opportunity every day to change our circumstances. You can have it all when you choose to keep fighting for what you want. Many people keep going after they fail a test multiple times. Why? It's something deep within their hearts and minds that won't allow them to give up on their dreams. Find that strength within yourself and keep fighting for your dreams.

Chapter Nine

Understand your Spiritual Warfare

When you think of the state of the world today, what comes up in your spirit? Fear. Anxiety. Depression. Suicidal ideation.

Each of these mentioned are on the rise in communities and homes across the world. When we begin to examine the impact of the pandemic more closely, we see a common denominator that our spirits are under attack.

Many of us are living in a constant state of fear and terror. We are constantly inundated with bad news of reports of war, poverty, mass shooting, unemployment, and much more. It's a lot to process all at once into our spirit. We are living in a time when our spirits are under constant attack.

The truth is that we are at war.

The war we fight is not of this world; it's of the spiritual realm.

Good and evil.

As we have progressed as a society, we must understand that the world has lost sight of core values and principalities. Today, we are encouraged to only think of ourselves and neglect those who are suffering in plain sight. Thus, our communities and homes are more encumbered with people who feel lost or misplaced among us.

When we speak of our spiritual wellness, we must begin to ask ourselves the things that our spirit needs to thrive. Our spirits need to thrive and exist within a world where we feel safe within our homes or churches. We need to be surrounded by community and friends who understand our pains and allow us to grow. Our spirits desire connection and touch because we are created to be in partnership. We are not designed to live in solitary forever.

> *"For where two or three are gathered together in my name, there am I in the midst of them"*

> **—Matthew 18:20**

We need each other now, more than ever.

Many people may not be aware of those who have our best interest at heart and those who wish to destroy us—spirits that fuel our purpose and spirits that work against it. When you truly open your mind to this concept, you stop taking so much that happens to you in life personally.

You also begin to shift your perspective of life. I had to understand that the spirit in my mother and grandmother would not allow them to love me properly. Even though we share the same blood and the same DNA, we are of different spirits. Yes, this was the spirit they chose; however, they are casualties of this warfare. They are fighting through their own storms. The sad part of it all is that we are all victims in one shape or form. They are products of a generational curse, and I am the change agent that is seen as unruly and out of line. I used to be so hurt and upset that I could not have the traditional love I saw my friends have with their mothers and grandmothers. But when I shifted my mind to grasp that I was indeed watching them lose their battles, I grew sad for them. I began to worry for their souls. I thought to myself about the pain they must feel to be moved to this level of harbored hatred. I have witnessed their spiritual sicknesses rob them of the blessings and joy that were right in front of them. Even now, I cry for them. My heart aches for them because I see the potential joy they could have if only they could see past their emotions and tap into their spiritual warrior.

When you are in a situation that does not feel right, move around! These are gifts of intuition and discernment that God gives to us to help protect ourselves. We strengthen these gifts by arming ourselves. How? We pray. We read and educate ourselves with scripture. We feed what we need to become stronger. We take daily steps that move the bigger picture, "Saving your soul." A very good close friend once told me, "The best thing you can do is find out God's plan and see how you can get on board." Now that looks different to everyone, but you get the point. That feeling in your stomach you can't explain when certain people come around makes you alert to their movement. Guard your peace and protect your crown at all costs. You don't need to share everything with everyone.

Take inventory of how people treat you when they don't think they need you. This is a perfect way for you to see a person's true colors, intentions, and true spirit.

Chapter Ten

Self-Reflection

Be prepared to ask and answer some hard truths about yourself

Self-reflection is an important part of personal growth. It helps you to become more self-aware and connect with your authentic self. This, in turn, allows you to step out of a life on autopilot so that you can start forging a path toward the things you want to achieve and the person you want to become. Self-reflection helps you adopt a more positive mindset too.

Instead of dwelling on the past, you'll find yourself spending more time looking forward, focusing on where you want to go and how you're going to get there. What has contributed most to my healing and growth is reflecting on where I see myself in the next few years. When we begin to envision our lives years ahead, we put ourselves in a better light. To help you become your best self in the coming years, I've included some self-reflection questions below.

Self-reflection questions about the past:

What battles have you fought and overcome in your life?

_____

_____

_____

What moments in your life are you most proud of so far?

_____

_____

_____

Which past experiences are you most thankful for?

_____

_____

_____

If you could turn back time, what would you do differently? Why?

_____

_____

_____

_____

What's the bravest thing you've ever done?

_____

_____

When we revisit our past, it's not to bring up bad memories or the people that caused us pain. It reminds us that we have gone through a human experience and prepared us for today. Don't allow your past to control your present. Be reminded that once you were a different version of the woman you are now. There was a time in your life when things didn't make sense and you struggled. There was a time in your life when you didn't know how to achieve clarity and peace. Now, you do.

Our past may be ugly, filled with dark secrets, tragedy, and pain. When we were at our lowest moments, we didn't know how we were going to move past the worst. Somehow, life gave us a second chance to make things right. That's how you should look at your past today. Don't blame yourself for things you didn't know. You had to learn through life experience in order to become who you are today. You are not a prisoner of your past choices, decisions, or situations. No one can walk in your shoes and live past what you have been through. They may not have survived. Congratulations on making it through every single hard day you have ever had. Allow your past to serve as a reminder that you might go through things, but you have the willpower to make tomorrow much better. As long as you're striving towards your best self, you will face many obstacles. The difference is now you are becoming more prepared and equipped to handle life's curveballs. Don't be afraid to start over because now, you have bigger tools to build a bigger house. Brick by brick and step by step, build your warrior within.

Self-reflection questions for your present:

What season of your life are you in right now?

_____

_____

_____

What are your top priorities?

_____

_____

_____

What takes up the majority of your time?

_____

_____

_____

Which aspects of your life are you able to control?

_____

_____

_____

What area of your life needs the most improvement?

_____

_____

_____

How are you making progress toward your goals?

_____

_____

_____

When we talk about our lives in the present, it's like a highlight reel. We want everyone around us to focus on the good stuff. The good might include a new marriage, a milestone birthday, starting a business, or getting a promotion at work. The good parts of our lives are easier to show to those around us. We often seek other people's approval and validation that we are doing good in our journey. The truth of the matter is, we don't have to focus on just the good stuff. The good parts make us feel warm and fuzzy on the inside. It's a dream or accomplishment realized before our eyes. Yet, our lives are not perfect by any means. We want to believe that if we achieve one or two major life goals, that's it. Life is going to be smooth sailing from this point. It's not true.

Our lives are a constant work in progress even in the present. The present is truly a gift because it reflects our hard work paying off. Being present is also about understanding the value of focusing on the person you want to become. None of us are perfect. We're all in different chapters of our journey. Your chapter five doesn't look like someone else's chapter twenty. The present is an opportunity to express gratitude for all that you have worked towards. Don't beat yourself up if you're not a millionaire by thirty or famous at fifty.

Our present is a reflection of our life choices whether those choices have opened up more doors of opportunity or taught us valuable life lessons to prepare us for what we want. Don't take any moments for granted. The present is the best gift you can ever receive.

Self-reflection questions about your future:

What does your ideal/dream life look like?

_____

_____

_____

What's on your bucket list?

_____

_____

_____

If you had the chance, what would you tell your future self?

_____

_____

_____

If you only had one year left to live, what would you do and whom would you tell? If anyone, Why did you choose the people you chose?

_____

_____

_____

If you met your future self, what questions would you ask?

_____

_____

_____

When I think of the future, it brings joy to my eyes. I envision myself further along in my career. My family is happy and healthy. My business is growing, and I'm financially stable. It's not a dream; it's my truth. When we think of the future, too often, it seems so far away. The future begins tomorrow. Tomorrow is a day we have never seen or experienced. Yet, we envision this day to be better than the last.

Our future self is waiting for us to answer the call to live out our dreams, not fears. Be inspired to dream big, bold, and in color when it comes to living out your dreams. The only limit is the limit you put on yourself. Could you imagine what the world would look like if people like Beyonce, Serena Williams, or Michelle Obama decided not to think about their future? Allow the accomplishments of others to motivate you to make your dreams not only a part of your future but your reality.

Self-reflection questions about personal growth:

If you could only use five words, how would you describe yourself?

_____

_____

_____

What are you most grateful for?

_____

_____

_____

What qualities do you admire in others that you wish you could see in yourself?

_____

_____

_____

What did you learn about yourself this past year?

_____

_____

_____

What are some of your short and long-term goals?

_____

_____

_____

Personal growth is defined by intentional actions to deliberately improve oneself. Your personal growth is not defined by your friends, peers, or relatives. Your personal growth is just for you. Don't attach your growth to a trend or influencer. You must be willing to step into your healing and grow. When you begin to embark on this journey of personal growth, you'll find yourself questioning everything you once knew. That's okay.

Sometimes, we must bury the parts of ourselves that are no longer serving the person we want to become. Don't try to rush through your personal growth process. It's going to get ugly before it gets beautiful. When you take time to examine your thoughts, habits, and choices, you give yourself room to break generational cycles and poverty mindsets. When you become your best self, you have the power to walk into your abundance and destiny with your head held high.

Before you close this book and jump into a new episode of your favorite show, I want to encourage you to take a little more time with these questions. Go beyond these questions and ask yourself more. Discover parts of yourself that you may have forgotten after becoming a mom or wife. You deserve to find out different parts of yourself to love and appreciate all that life has to offer. Yes, we get busy, and things happen in our lives that are beyond our control. I want to remind you that the things you learn about yourself in your personal growth journey will prepare you for moments of uncertainty and discomfort.

Chapter Eleven

True Self-love

Someone once asked, "If you could name all the people you love ... how long would it take for you to name yourself?"

When we think about love, we know it to be a feeling of joy and affection for another being. Many of us never come to understand the power of self-love. We begin our dating journey in pursuit of someone to love us the way we imagine it's supposed to be. How are people supposed to love us? For many of us, we give our love away in relationships. It quickly becomes a game of how can I get this person to love me and no one else. Thus, you begin showering people with gifts or money. In the long run, you begin to feel like the love you seek is not real or obtainable. The kind of love you desire can only exist within a Hollywood film. The truth is, the love that you willingly give to others begins with you.

You're the key to receiving the kind of love you want from others. That kind of love is called self-love. We're not taught self-love in school or the media. Oftentimes, we learn about self-love through self-help books, friendship, or in counseling. By those points, you've experienced a lot of pain, rejection, and disappointment when it comes to love. Let's talk a little more about self-love.

Self-love is not exclusively about rewarding yourself with lavish gifts or frequent vacations. That's on the other side of self-love. Self-love is understanding that loving yourself from a healthy place begins with you. When you love yourself, you speak positively to yourself. You don't focus on the things you don't like about yourself. You work on intentionally improving yourself with fitness, education, and trying new things. When you begin to love yourself for who you are, you interact with others differently. When we love ourselves, we will not allow others to disrespect or abuse us. Self-love helps us to establish healthy boundaries with our family, friends, and partners.

When we learn about self-love, it's from other people's perspectives. Your mom may tell you that you don't love yourself if you don't go shopping. Your best friend may mention that if you don't keep up your appearances. Your partner may begin to neglect you if you put on weight. When people notice things about us in the way we care for ourselves, it can hurt. Self-love is not just about a new wardrobe, manicure, or exercise routine. Self-love begins with how you feel about yourself day to day. Do you feel motivated to get out of bed in the morning? Are you happy with your job? Are you in a relationship that contributes to your well-being?

These are questions we have to ask ourselves periodically. It's important to check in with yourself and understand why you're feeling this way. When we love ourselves, we understand that putting ourselves in unhealthy environments could affect our mental health.

When you have people in your life that belittle you or constantly remind you of why you're not capable of success, it has a direct impact on how you treat and talk to yourself. It's pivotal in our upbringing to learn how to love ourselves and not seek validation from others. You can learn to implement self-love into your life in a few ways, such as:

- Keeping a journal of your daily/monthly goals
- Write down quotes or phrases that inspire you
- Associate yourself with other successful people
- Watch motivational videos
- Follow social media accounts that inspire you
- Try yoga or meditation to center your thoughts
- Get active in your community
- Reward yourself when you reach milestones
- Write positive affirmations on a post-it
- Write down all the reasons you love yourself
- Remove negativity from your life

We often hear people say, "Self-love begins with you," it really does. When you love who you are you won't lower your standards, you'll be prepared to handle love and all its many curveballs. Self-love is standing in the mirror in your birthday suit and loving what you see. You may have bumps, dimples, cellulite, and love handles. That's okay. That just means your body has changed over time, and you survived. Don't speak negatively to yourself because you're the first person to hear it. You also permit other people to speak to you in the same manner.

Our journey in life is filled with many obstacles and roadblocks. We need people and moments in our life to frequently remind us that life is worth living. Life is a journey of self-discovery and serving God. God wants to bless us beyond our prayer request. We have to trust in Him always to exceed our expectations. We have to be grateful for all things that He is doing in our lives.

You can live your best life with what you have today, and God will bless you with more. A painful past does not disqualify you from a beautiful future.

God's Plan for You Begins with Clarity

Clarity: We lose sight of where we are going on our journey many times. Our thoughts and intentions come out of alignment with God's word and direction for our lives. In challenging times, we must seek clarity. Clarity begins when we can look within ourselves and ask, "What do I want?" Being able to ask yourself the clear question of what you want in every area of your life is vital. The conversations that we have with ourselves daily is essential to how we define our life. You have to be open and honest with yourself about your choices. If the choices you are making are leaving you in a state of despair and confusion, it's time to make a change. Gaining clarity allows you to refocus and pursue the life you desire with a purpose. Get clear about what you want, and you are going to create the life you desire. God will match your vision for your life and begin to direct your path.

Find Purpose: Oftentimes, we hear experts and counselors refer to defining your purpose in life as the secret to happiness. Unfortunately, discovering your purpose is not as easy as listening to someone share their philosophy of a purpose-filled life. What is the purpose? Purpose is your motivation to keep going when you've been let down numerous times. Purpose is the fire in your spirit when you are doing something you love. Purpose is to fight for what you believe in because it inspires you to make an impact. Too often, we go through life trying to attach our purpose to our jobs, relationships, bank account, or status in the communities we serve. The source of our purpose is not defined by how we make a living or titles. You define your purpose by asking yourself tough questions and honoring the truth about yourself. If what you love to do could be free and still positively make an impact on society, you've discovered the reason you're here.

Find passion: The secret to wealth and happiness is passion. What are you good at? What do you love to do? Many of us find passion in writing music, painting, singing, dancing, and more. The question is, "Could you do all those things that bring you joy and get paid for it?" Today, we are seeing a rise in serial entrepreneurs on social media. Why? Because more people are discovering ways to get paid to do what they love daily. It's not just about surviving to pay bills and rent any longer. We live in a society that promotes entrepreneurship and pursuing your passion while earning a profit. You can be passionate about your hobbies and create a lifestyle that supports your family.

Support: Oftentimes, during our journey of life, we will evolve into someone we do not recognize. Evolution is necessary for our growth and sustainability. However, once we start on a new path, we often find it challenging to garner support. Finding yourself in a busy world is not easy. We want all of our friends and family's support when we start a business, go back to school, or have kids. Support may not often come packaged as you perceive it to be. Support can come from a friend who buys your products or word of mouth about your business. You may not have five or six people in your corner when you start a new chapter in your life. Don't be discouraged by the lack of support. Be encouraged that God has you on a special assignment, and He will support you along the way.

Career Choice & Income: Back in school, most of us look forward to career day. This was the day members of the community came in to talk about their careers. This was an instrumental moment in many of our lives in childhood. Why? Because we had a representation of fulfilling our dreams and what was possible for our future. Choosing a career that is fulfilling for your life path is an imperative choice. The career you choose could lead you into a lifestyle that will reward you with a lucrative income. Determining the type of income you would like to accumulate over time should contribute to a comfortable lifestyle. An important fact to mention is managing your finances as you accumulate wealth. Financial education will increase your awareness of how you feel about yourself and your life.

Never Stop Growing: As we grow older, we must be open-minded to adjusting to learning in different ways. Most of us associate the learning chapter of our life to be complete after graduation. That's actually not true. Although our formative years are influential in teaching us about the world we exist within, the real education begins with our life experiences and challenges. Whether you're striving to understand how technology has changed and impacted our lives in a positive way or understanding love, you must adapt to learning daily in a fast-paced world. Seeking knowledge on the path of fulfilling your life destiny requires spending time in self-development.

Love Thy Self: How many times do you say, "I love you" to yourself? Think about it. We often find it much easier to express our love and admiration for others than we do ourselves. The love that we willingly and frequently give to others begins with the love we give to ourselves. Learning to love yourself is more than just catering to your outer appearance or splurging on lavish gifts. Self-love begins with embracing the person in the mirror. How do you talk to yourself? Your conversations with yourself should be uplifting and positive. You should feel empowered to see yourself healthy and thriving in a growing world where your voice matters. Don't compare yourself to others. God made you just the way He intended. Love yourself from the inside out. You have so much love to offer the world. Take some time to love yourself first.

Forgive: When people that we love disappoint, betray, or harm us, we find it hard to forgive them. Love begins with trust. We trust the people we love to never do anything that would make us question their role in our lives. The truth of the matter is, people are going to let you down. They are going to break your heart and walk out of your life without warning. We cannot control other people. We can control if we choose to forgive them. Forgiveness is not for the other person. It's really for you. When we carry the burden of the pain that someone else has caused, we give that person control over our emotions and actions. No one should have that much power over you. Forgiveness makes you stronger and frees you from holding on to the past. We all make mistakes and fall short of other people's expectations. You would want someone else to forgive you for your shortcomings. Put yourself in their shoes and allow forgiveness to teach how to heal a relationship.

Health: On average, we eat more fast food than greens and fruit. Why? For one, fast food places are on every corner of our neighborhoods. When we're hungry for a quick bite, we gravitate towards something that will satisfy our hunger in minutes. Unfortunately, too much fast food is harmful to the body. We honor our temple by eating clean and nourishing our organs with vitamins and veggies. Although our fast food habits are conducive to a fast-paced lifestyle and world, we have to start thinking long-term about where we want to be within our health. Moving your body frequently and eating a well-balanced meal regularly develops a healthy habit. If you take care of your body today, your body will take care of you.

Reward Small Wins: We ignore the small wins that lead to big victories too often. Society teaches us to only focus on the big picture. We definitely don't want to lose sight of our goals and dreams. However, it's important to acknowledge your hard work and small victories along the way. The road to success is not a sprint, it's a marathon. You will need to stop and enjoy the view along the way. Reward the small wins, break down the big wins, and brick by brick—step by step—walk, crawl, and run. Please don't skip this order.

Your best life begins with falling in love and appreciation for what you already have today. Don't compare your chapter ten to someone else's chapter thirty. It takes time and consistency to create the life of your dreams. Every day is an opportunity to make better choices to live the life of your dreams. When we honor all that God has blessed us with today, we make room for Him to bless us abundantly. So many people are counting their blessings because they have less than you. Before you describe your life as bad, think about the person sleeping underneath the bridge, the single mom who doesn't have enough food to feed her family, or the man or woman who just received a diagnosis of a terminal illness. Life is short. Don't define it by comparing it to someone else. Live your best life by having gratitude for the simple things.

Before you give your heart and commitment to loving someone else, love yourself first. Don't jump into a relationship because you're lonely or afraid of being single. Women who love themselves understand that loving themselves is more important than rushing into a relationship. A relationship is a commitment, and it's the step before marriage. Take your time and get to know yourself. We allow societal standards to get inside our heads and make us question our self-worth. Stop it! Just because you're not married with kids or dating in your forties does not mean you don't deserve love. You can have an even better love story when you've taken the time to get to know yourself.

When we understand who we are and what we bring to the table, we don't bargain or compromise for less than we deserve. Self-love is about understanding that you are enjoying your time with God. You're allowing God to develop you into the woman He has called you to be. When you trust God in every area of your life, you can never go wrong. Love yourself more than you love the desire to validate love's presence in your life.

Chapter Twelve

Speak up

DON'T SETTLE.

Those were the words I recite to myself in any situation I feel uncertain about. As a black woman, people are accustomed to me giving pushback and getting an attitude. It's not an attitude that bothers me. It's the blatant disrespect that society has for women when it comes to women of color.

We're told to settle for less money, poor schools, being unlovable, hard to work with, etc. I've had my share of settling for one life too many. I've learned that you don't have to settle for anything less than the best. We are living in a time when we as women of color can demand more money, hold others accountable for mistreating us, negotiate our terms, and start our own businesses. Why not ask for the forty acres and a mule?

Don't be afraid to ask for what you want. People will always give you what they think you deserve. You have to learn to fight back and stand your ground. It may be hard, and you might even want to fold under the pressure. Don't! When you fight for a little more money or a promotion, you send a message across industries and the world.

Your message is that you deserve the power and respect that comes with the territory as much as the next person.

We have to be cognizant of what we are teaching our daughters. We need them to know that just because you are a woman in a male-dominated industry doesn't mean you can't be the boss. You can be all that and more.

For many generations, black women have adopted a fear and mentality that we must settle for what we can get. We watched as our mothers, grandmothers, aunts, and neighbors worked their whole lives for a little bit of something. With the little that they had, they managed to help inspire future generations to strive for more. We owe it to ourselves and our elders to push past the limits of racism and inequality. We are our ancestors living dreams, and that is a responsibility to be proud of. We have to find the strength to reclaim what is rightfully ours.

We must always keep in mind that the next generation is watching and waiting. We must work hard to give them a fighting chance, to give them a future they can inherit with dignity and pride.

Chapter Thirteen

Faith

"I believed that there was a God because I was told it by my grandmother and later by other adults. But when I found that I knew not only that there was God but that I was a child of God, when I understood that, when I comprehended that, more than that, when I internalized that, ingested that, I became courageous."

—Maya Angelou

I titled this book "Through the Storm" because many of us are fighting some type of storm in our lives. The storm may represent a divorce, an illness, job loss, or financial hardship. I want to end the book with words of encouragement. I want to encourage you to build your muscle. I want to encourage you to feed your warrior. Life will take you through many storms. Hold your head up and warrior them.

You may have seen the storm coming and thought it would pass you by. You may have seen the storm heading in your direction and didn't know what to do until it was too late. No matter where you are in the storm, I want you to know there is life on the other side. If you are reading this book, realize that you have survived every single hard day you have ever had.

We all faced the uncertainty of COVID-19, massive job loss, and countless deaths. It was hard to keep the faith with a lot of devastation all around us. Many of us took the quarantine to rediscover the meaning of life and reconnect with God. The year was quite difficult to process on our own. Many of us didn't know how we were going to feed our families or maintain a roof over our heads.

Here we are today, standing on the other side of that storm. Many of us thought we'd never live to see this day. What does the other side look like to you?

The other side may look different than what you're used to. You might overcome your illness but have to be dependent on someone else. You might have to take a job with less pay. You may have to relocate to another city or town. When you make it to the other side, you should feel a sense of relief and joy. The storm was never meant to break you; it was meant to make you stronger. Many people wonder why God takes us through so many storms in our lives. I believe that God puts us through storms to teach us lessons we will need later in life and test our faith and love for Him. He wants to know that we are truly ready for what we've been asking for in our lives. Some of us get greedy and become unhappy with the things God has given us. You're not happy with your three-bedroom house. You believe you deserve a five-bedroom house with a bigger mortgage. Are you ready to manage and maintain all that comes with a five-bedroom house? Have you shown God that you can handle and appreciate a little? None of us are perfect. God doesn't want us to suffer. He doesn't want to punish us. He doesn't want us to be without His promise. God wants all the glory and the praise while you're in the trenches and the fight of your life. Just because He blesses us with our hearts' desires doesn't mean we get to ask for more than we deserve. A lot of times, we get exactly what we want and begin to neglect God.

The truth of the matter is, we can't replace God in our lives with material things. Sometimes, as people, we make it to the height of success and leave God behind. Our success is nothing without the will of God attached to it.

We don't have time to serve, give back, help our communities, or acknowledge God's presence in our lives. We're too busy. We're living our best life and enjoying the fruits of our labor. But when God takes us through circumstance and difficulty, we run towards him for help. We need Him to hurry up and answer our prayers. God doesn't work like that.

God wants us to have an intimate relationship with Him. He doesn't want us to shut Him out of our thoughts and decisions. God wants to guide us through life's difficult moments. When I was going through my job layoff, it was hard for me to open up to God. I was battling with so much pain and anger inside myself that it was hard for me to breathe. I was trying to deal with everything on my own. I needed help in ways that only God could answer. I've always been a woman of faith. But at times, my faith was tested by what was happening in my life. It was hard for me to submit or surrender it all to God. I wanted to go out and figure things out for myself. I had to accept there was very little I could do to change my situation back to the way things were before the pandemic. I wanted a part of my life back where things actually made sense. I had a sense of control over the things that were happening in my life. When I lost my job and identity, it was hard in the beginning to turn toward God.

Even in my most difficult moments, I knew God was still within me. There was no way I had enough strength on my own. He was just waiting for me to come to Him. When life gets hard, we must remember not to fold under the pressure. The pressure will cause you to question if God is real or if God can help change your situation. In those times, you must silence all of the background noise in your head and lean on God.

God wants us to be obedient to His word. Your relationship with God should be ongoing throughout all the days of your life. When God takes us through the storm, He's right by our side holding our hands. He hasn't forgotten you when you go through an eviction, job loss, or lose a loved one. Sometimes, we get so caught up in the situation that we miss the lesson. God is right there when it is happening. He wants us to trust Him. Trust Him with our heart's desires, darkest secrets, deepest fears, insecurities, and weaknesses. God can handle it all.

We all come to the point in our lives when we need a little help to make it through our crisis. Oftentimes, God sends His angels on earth to guide us back into His kingdom. Sometimes, that help doesn't look like the people we trust the most. It could be your neighbor, nurse, or the good Samaritan that helps you on the side of the road. I want you to know that you're not alone in your storm. Don't be too proud to ask for help. God wants to send people into your life that will not judge you, but that will offer you a helping hand in times of tragedy.

We are not perfect people. Many of us are struggling with demons from our past and the ones we invited inside. When you don't know whom to trust in your life, ask God for discernment. God will reveal to you the people in your life that are doing you the most harm. Discernment is there for your protection to help you understand God's love for you. God would never turn His back on you. He is always there when you need Him, day or night.

My prayer for you as you move into the next chapter of your life is to move with love and kindness. Many of us are focused on the next best thing or whom we can get over in life. Don't live your life in such a way that dishonors you and displeases God. We are all going through a storm, heading towards one, or coming out of a storm. Be loving and supportive of those around you. They may need a shoulder to cry on or a listening ear. We all can become a better version of ourselves each day. Love yourself as God loves you. Remember that the storm won't last forever, but the love of God will always be available.

www.ingramcontent.com/pod-product-compliance
Lightning Source LLC
Chambersburg PA
CBHW070443130626
46553CB00006B/2284